BEST
IMPRESSIONS

How to Gain
PROFESSIONALISM
PROMOTION
and
PROFIT

By Dawn E. Waldrop

First Edition
Cleveland, Ohio

Inquiries should be addressed to:
Best Impressions®, 17749 Lexington Lane, Cleveland, Ohio 44136.

Published Cleveland, Ohio

Printed in the U.S.A.
First Printing: January 1997

Printer: BookMasters, Inc. / BookCrafters
Cover design: Deloitte & Touche LLP, Terry Kammer & Francine Hamper
Cover Photographs: Judi Terrill Linden Photography
Copy Editor: Margaret Friedrich

Library of Congress Catalog Card Number: 96-95141

ISBN 0-9655742-3-7

Table of Contents

Acknowledgments

About the Author

Introduction

Acknowledgments

I want to thank the following people for their contribution and support to make this book a success.

My husband, **James**,
for all his support and patience.

My son, **Greg Stroemple II**,
who is my "best impression."

My sister-in-law and copy editor, **Margaret Friedrich,**
for her countless hours of editing.

My friend, **Mari Beth Gavlak**,
who inspired me to this career.

I dedicate this book to

My deceased father
who would be proud.

My grandson, **Adam Gregory Christian**
and my nephew, **Brian**,
may they both benefit from this book.

About the Author

Dawn E. Waldrop is the President and founder of Best Impressions® in Cleveland, Ohio. As a national speaker, trainer and author she educates men and women on how to project their professional **best**.

Professional image development is an educational skill that can be mastered by any man or woman willing to learn. However, this complete learning process is not provided in the educational institutions. Professional image development is not about making you something you are not, putting you in clothes you are uncomfortable in or taking away your favorite outfits. It is exactly the opposite. Image development is about showing you what works **best for you** in color, fit, textures, patterns, accessories, grooming techniques, industry and career position.

Dawn is seen on television, heard on radio and her written word is read nationally on professional image development. Thousands of men and women have enjoyed learning from Dawn how to utilize their appearance as a positive business tool.

She has trained employees of Fortune 500 companies: Merrill Lynch, Praxair, New York Life Ins., KeyCorp, Banc One Corp, Marriott Int'l, Progressive Ins. & Parker Hannifin. NASA, Geon Co., and Case Western Reserve University are among the clients that have benefited from her expertise. Her speaking presentations and training programs are interactive and fun because Dawn delivers this educational content with energy, stories and audience involvement.

Introduction

For centuries people wore no clothes. Body ornamentation or decorative shells, nose rings, earrings, body piercing and body painting preceded wearing clothes. The invention and evolution of clothes began with loin cloths or wrapped thongs.

The apron was worn which became a skirt, then trousers. Furs were worn as cloaks. Grasses or materials created skirts worn with head, neck and arm ornaments.

People could express their sexuality, culture, religion, government position or individuality through clothes. "Clothes make the man" became the saying. Special costumes were designed for celebrations like Mardi Gras. Movie actors dressed in costume to represent the character they were playing.

We found clothes affect how we feel about ourselves and how others perceive us. Clothes universally communicate who we are and what we want to accomplish. The trend shifted from conformity to non-conformity in clothing attire.

In the business environment the style evolved from the company uniform, to a business suit uniform, to almost anything goes in work attire. Today and for years to come, working men and women can learn to be their own person, yet project a professional, fine-tuned appearance.

Two individuals can dress differently yet project their professional best. After all, we are not all cut from the same cloth. This book will show you how to develop your *best professional style*!

❖

Chapter One

Looking "Okay" or Looking Your "Best"

Does this sound familiar to you? You get up in the morning, get dressed and go to work. All day you feel something is not quite right with your outfit. You do not feel comfortable. When you get home you immediately change into different clothes. You notice that your day went right along with how you felt about your appearance, just "okay."

Have you not had other days, though, when you got up, got dressed, went to work and you felt your "best" in the outfit you wore? When you got home, you were not in a hurry to change your clothes because you felt great and your day was very productive as well.

While growing up, both men and women devote time trying to appear fashionable. Just buying the latest fashions is not the best preparation for building a professional wardrobe.

Buying the latest fashions is not the best preparation for building a professional wardrobe.

Men and women today do not have time to put the effort or money into developing their wardrobes. They are tired of wasting money on clothes and accessories which sit in the closet.

The image you project influences the opinion of others and how you feel about yourself.

The professional world has made attention to dress important to the success level of our career. This is due to economic changes; we have become a more service-oriented country and the working population continues to grow. More service jobs require a professional wardrobe instead of a uniform traditionally required in a manufacturing environment. Growth in the working population has increased competition for jobs.

Knowing how to look your professional best is a very persuasive tool in the business world. Fifty-five percent of how you are perceived is through the visual messages you project through your appearance. This image influences the opinion of others as well as how you feel about yourself. In business, you dress to have an impact on the people around you. If your appearance conveys a negative message, it becomes extremely difficult to overcome the negative signals from your attire. In employment interviews, research has shown most hiring decisions are made within the first five minutes of the interview. By projecting your professional best you show respect for yourself and those around you.

By projecting your professional best you show respect for yourself and those around you.

Your visual presence must have integrity and consistency. Looking professional is a skill that can be mastered by any man or woman who wants to learn it. Those men and women who invest time to develop "appearance as a tool" have greater impact and professional credibility. You need to get dressed everyday. Why look "okay," when you can **learn** to look your **best** with less time, effort and money?

*Those men and women who invest time to develop "**appearance as a tool**" have greater impact and professional credibility.*

Take this quiz to see how much you know about professional image development.

Professional Image Quiz

---

1. *Your professional attire should be ____% of your closet.*

   a. 30%   b. 70%   c. 55%

2. *What is the most professional outfit?*

   a. business suit all one color

   b. blazer different color from skirt/trouser pants

   c. long sleeve shirt/blouse with trouser pants/skirt

3. *What does a professional **casual** outfit consist of?*

   a. short sleeve shirt/blouse with trouser pants

   b. blazer, shirt/blouse with trouser pants

   c. business suit, jacket different color than skirt or pants

4. ___% *of companies today will not hire, promote or keep individuals who do not project a positive professional appearance.*

    a. 50%   b. 70%   c. 90%

5. *How should you dress at work to gain respect and recognition?*

    a. one level better than current position

    b. same job level as everyone else

    c. a job level less than current position

6. *What is the first and last item of your appearance people see?*

    a. hair   b. shoes   c. face

7. *The tip of a man's tie should hit*

    a. above the belt

    b. middle of the belt

    c. below the belt

8. *Shoe color should be the ___ than your hemline.*

    a. same color as your hair

    b. same color or darker

    c. lighter

9. *What is an important yet overlooked accessory for a man?*

   a. shoes

   b. watch

   c. briefcase

10. *___ is the appropriate dress or skirt length for a woman.*

    a. middle of the knee

    b. two or more inches above the knee

    c. two or more inches below the knee

11. *What is the most important, yet neglected, accessory for men and women?*

    a. shoes   b. jewelry   c. briefcase

Answers:

1. **(b)** People spend the majority of their day at work.

2. **(a)** Business suit creates most authority.

3. **(b)** This is *business casual* for most jobs.

4. **(b)** Companies want professionals who dress the part and look like a professional.

5. **(a)** People remember you.

6. **(b)** We look at people from the feet to the face when they enter a room. We look at people from the head to the feet when they leave a room.

7. **(b)** The tie tip above or below the belt buckle appears not to fit.

8. **(b)** When shoes are a lighter color than the hemline we see the feet and not the face.

9. **(b)** Men often wear a watch too casual.

10. **(a)** Middle of the knee works best and you do not have to worry about fashion lengths.

11. **(a)** Shoes are the first and last item we see.

How did you score?

Chapter Two

Benefits, Benefits, Benefits

Ninety percent of the population cannot put themselves together to look their best. Why is this? The answer is at no time in the educational system are we taught how to do this. Men and women are realizing that image development is something that must be learned, just as we learn job skills. If you did not learn how to read or write, what do you think would happen? You would muddle through, trial and error...correct? Isn't that what we do with our appearance? We follow fashion or catch can. Sometimes it works. Most of the time it does not, especially with our professional wardrobe.

Men and women are realizing that image development is something that must be learned, just as we learn job skills.

You have worked hard to develop your job skills. You do not want to miss out on an opportunity because of your wardrobe, grooming or accessories. Count on these truths: To gain respect, dress as well as or one step better than your industry standard. To obtain a promotion, look the part for the position you desire. Dress for the position you seek, not the position you currently hold.

Benefit One: *By looking your best, your confidence and productivity level increase.*

Your total appearance package projects who you are, how you feel about yourself, and how you will perform on the job.

Your total appearance package projects who you are, how you feel about yourself and how you will perform on the job. Remember those mornings when you felt one hundred percent comfortable in your attire and your day was productive as well? You felt good, your self esteem and confidence were at high levels. Hundreds of research studies have proven when an individual looks their **professional** best, they in turn feel their best and their productivity level increases. You are productive when your energies are focused on your work and not on what you are wearing that day. Whenever you are self-conscious about an article of clothing or accessory, it reduces your productivity.

Conversely, self-confidence generates increased productivity, efficiency and profitability.

Benefit Two: *By looking your professional best, you gain respect and recognition.*

Just as you cannot skip a skill to perform your job, you cannot overlook your image.

Your total image gives you a distinct advantage and is the single most important non-verbal communication cue you give about yourself. By projecting your professional best, those people around you give you the respect and recognition you deserve. They see you respect yourself by the time you take with your appearance. In the business world, employers will offer you more opportunities to grow with the company. Your appearance is a piece of the total skill package in the work world. Just as you cannot skip a skill to perform your job, you cannot overlook your image.

Benefit Three: *By looking your best consistently, success comes more quickly and gives you security.*

Your appearance is a tool which can be used to your advantage to better your career. This tool gives you a competitive edge in the professional market. Those who invest time to develop appearance as a tool have greater impact and professional credibility. Credibility drives opportunity which drives increased income. You are not only selling a service, product or performing a job for the employer, you are selling yourself.

Your appearance is a tool which gives you a competitive edge in the job market.

Be aware that you are viewed as a professional. Make the effort to project that professional image at **all** times. With all the changes taking place in companies, management looks to keep only those employees who have a complete, consistent professional appearance package. This package consists of appearance, communication, human relation and technical skills.

You are not only selling a service, product or performing a job for the employer, you are selling yourself.

Benefit Four: *By planning ahead it takes less effort to dress your best.*

Just as you have a career plan, you need to have an image plan. Your image plan involves the same commitment that you devote to any other aspect of your life. Just as it took time to learn your job skills, the same applies to your wardrobe skills. On average, it takes two years to pull together a complete wardrobe. After learning what colors, styles, materials and designs work **best** for you, you then can develop a wardrobe plan. Your wardrobe plan will automatically develop into a shopping plan. Purchase items which project your **best** image and slowly filter out those clothes or accessories which do not.

Benefit Five: *It takes less time to look your professional best.*

Once your image plan is completed and in effect you never have to spend time contemplating what to wear.

You will *always* have shoes and combinations of outfits that go together without any effort or thought.

Benefit Six: *You do not have to spend a lot of money to look your best.*

Once you learn what works best for you in color, style, material and design you will not waste money on clothes or accessories. When you buy an article of clothing which does not enhance your coloring, body structure or personality, you feel uncomfortable. People can tell when you are uncomfortable. Those are the times you do not get complimented. Those are the clothes that go into the depths of the closet not to be worn again. Do you get rid of those clothes? Of course not, you spent good money on those clothes. Even if you spent only ten dollars on an article of clothing and do not wear it, that is like throwing ten dollars away.

You, too, can experience all the benefits of developing your best professional image. The visual package projected by you is a reflection of who you are, what you think about yourself as well as what type of job you will do for others. Appearance awareness is a vital component to your career success.

The visual package projected by you is a reflection of who you are, what you think about yourself as well as what type of job you will do for others.

When people meet you, they unconsciously form an instant opinion of you. This process is a part of human nature and will never change. In those first few seconds they decide if you are trustworthy, successful, what your moral character is, your age, as well as your educational, economic, professional and social position. To be a successful professional you obviously want those decisions to be favorable. Once you realize how much the messages perceived by others is based on your appearance, you will quickly learn to be more aware of your outward appearance. Realize the positive. An image that works for **you** helps you become the **best** professional you can be.

Appearance awareness is a vital component to your career success.

Chapter Three

What Do They See When They See You Coming?

Seventy percent of your wardrobe should be your work attire. Where are you the majority of the day? Men and women spend most of the day at their jobs. That is the reason why your professional wardrobe should be the majority of your closet. Twenty five percent of your wardrobe should be casual and five percent should be evening attire.

Seventy percent of your wardrobe should be your work attire.

Professional attire is made up of a **separate wardrobe**, not to be worn in a casual or evening situation. Do not interchange these wardrobes for work. For example: A man's business suit should not be worn with a pair of penny loafers or sports watch. A woman's business dress should not be worn with an open-toed, four-inch heel shoe.

The type of industry you are in will determine the **level** of appropriate professional attire. A detailed explanation of the levels of dress will follow on the next pages. Industries such as banking, financing, insurance, real estate, sales, management, business owner and all

The type of industry you are in will determine the **level** *of appropriate professional attire.*

professions which deal with people on a very personal, financial or emotional level require **level one** and **level two** of professional dress. **Level three** and **level four** of professional dress apply to clerical, secretarial, staff positions, service positions dealing face to face with the public or co-workers. **Level five** and **level six** apply to a professional casual industry such as creative industries (e.g. advertising), technical (e.g. computer database input or factory) or if a company has professional casual days, business seminars or business casual socials.

How others perceive you is in your control.

Employees should dress for the position they seek, not the position they currently hold, just as business owners should dress for the type of clientele they desire. Think about what image you want to project. How do you want others to perceive you? How others perceive you is in your control. Think about what type of industry you are in and the type of people with whom you come in contact. Then apply the appropriate level of dress from the following level descriptions.

Power Professional

Level One: Power Professional dress is a conservative long sleeve business suit for a man or woman. The same color jacket and pants for the man and a jacket and skirt for the woman will create the most business like appearance. The business suit projects the most authority. A white or cream shirt with a tie for the man and a white or cream blouse with simple accessories for the woman is the most professional. The business suit in a neutral color which is complementary to your personal coloring will work best. Neutrals are navy, gray, beige and brown. (See the chapter on color to learn your best colors.)

The business suit creates the most authority.

Professional

Level Two: Professional dress is a long sleeve business suit for the man and a long or short sleeve business suit for the woman. The jacket and pants or skirt may be a different color; for example, a charcoal jacket with a lighter gray pair of pants or skirt. Women will find more suits come with different color jackets and skirts, where men actually buy the jackets and pants separately and interchange them. Be careful in combining separates that you do not mix two totally different materials or patterns that do not coordinate. Women have more light and bright color choices. Color choices for the woman provide the opportunity to express femininity yet be professional. A woman **should** strive for a professional femininity. In the workplace men do not appreciate women trying to look like men. A woman will gain respect from the male gender by projecting a professional femininity.

Long sleeves create a sense of authority.

Level Three: Removing the jacket creates a more relaxed atmosphere and the third level of professionalism. A man with a shirt and tie with no jacket moves into level three. Level three for the woman is wearing a blouse and skirt combination or a professional dress. Long sleeves create a sense of authority. If the shirt, blouse or dress has short sleeves, you are creating a more relaxed situation.

Level Four: A man may wear a short sleeve shirt, pants and no tie. A woman may wear a short sleeve blouse with a skirt or professional dress.

Business Casual

Level Five: A man may wear a dark colored shirt or sweater with a pair of professional casual pants (100% cotton pleated style) with a pair of penny loafers. A woman may wear a blouse with a pair of professional casual pants (trouser style) and a pair of closed-in flat shoes.

Level Six: This level is only for the extremely creative fields such as an artist or for factory situations where no uniform is required. A clean, neat pair of jeans with clean, scuff free tennis shoes and a golf type shirt for the man or woman is very casual. Keep in mind these clothes are the most casual for business. By keeping your casual clothes separate from your professional casual wardrobe, they will last long-er, look neater and project a professional image.

By keeping your casual clothes separate from your professional casual wardrobe, they will last longer, look neater and project a professional image.

Level Five is how companies want their employees to dress when there is a casual day or business seminar. Unfortunately, most employees wear clothes they normally would wear outside of work to sport events, mowing the lawn or running errands. In reality the employer is asking you to dress one level lower than your normal professional attire. If you normally dress **Power Professional** then business casual for you is level two, three or four. Just as you want to recognize a service clerk, doctor, etc. as the professional, so do the people you come in contact with want to recognize you for the professional you are. There is a definite comfort level when we can visually recognize an individual as a professional.

Spend wisely on your professional wardrobe. **Think** about how many times you will wear that shirt or blouse to work. For example, you will wear a two hundred dollar business outfit on average 110 times over the life of the outfit. That comes to $1.80 per wearing. Compare that to a two hundred dollar evening outfit. Men will wear an evening outfit three times. A woman will wear an evening outfit one or two times. Now you are spending fifty to hundred dollars a wearing.

The Cost of Item divided by Number of Wearings equals Cost Per Wearing

Your clothes will last longer and you can purchase better quality if you follow this rule when shopping for your professional wardrobe:

Cost of Item ÷ Number of Wearings = Cost Per Wearing.

Good quality materials have fifty percent or more of a wool, cotton or silk blend. You will spend less money by investing in good quality blends of materials. One good quality suit or dress will last longer than three inexpensive suits or dresses.

One good quality suit or dress will last longer than three inexpensive suits or dresses.

THE PLAIN DEALER

Business

BY DAWN WALDROP

Dressing carefully can boost your credibility

One of the most difficult things to overcome in business is a negative first impression. After all, business relationships are based on a comfort and trust level that your customers seek, first of all, in your appearance.

Fifty-five percent of your first impression is a package deal: your clothing, grooming and accessories. Give yourself a competitive edge and market yourself visually. A strong professional image can result in new business and referral business, as well as maintaining existing business. Those who invest time to develop appearance as a tool have greater impact and professional credibility.

Here are some common mistakes that women make — and that if avoided, can enhance your credibility early on in your business relationships.

Worn or dirty shoes: Your shoes are the first and last item of your appearance people see; make sure they are always clean and not worn. Also, your shoe color should be the same color or darker than your hem line.

Not having your clothes tailored to fit: Clothes that do not fit properly look sloppy and project an image that you do not care and will not do a good job. Make sure the sleeves and hem lines are your correct length.

Improper business accessories: Carry a briefcase or business accessory. Make sure it is clean and not worn.

Your accessories are fine details. If you pay attention to details in your appearance, it projects the idea that you will pay attention to details in your job. Women should not carry a purse; it is not a professional accessory. Carry a briefcase, day timer or leather pad.

You also should never wear or carry plastic. Instead, wear a nice silver, gold or leather band watch. Carry a nice silver or gold pen.

Short sleeves during a presentation: Long sleeves give you a sense of authority. If you are in an important meeting or on a sales call, wear long sleeves. A suit jacket gives the most authority; next comes a long sleeve blouse or dress.

Not dressing for your appointments: Think about who you will be seeing that day, and dress appropriately. If one of your clients is a president or upper level manager, your dress dictates a business suit. If your next appointment is with a very casual company, you might try a removing your jacket from your business suit or dress.

On the other hand, however, just because your client is very casually dressed does not mean you can do the same. You always want to be recognized as the professional.

You also need to be prepared for any changes. Even your "dress-down" attire should be professional enough that, should you get an unexpected client appointment, you can pop on a jacket and look prepared.

And part of being so prepared lies in your having a wardrobe plan. Seventy-five percent of your closet should be your professional attire.

Waldrop is a professional speaker, trainer and consultant. She is president of Best Impressions.

Chapter Four

Credibility Enhancers & Robbers

Professional image is a tool that can advance your career. In today's world, time is of great value. By knowing how to project your best professional image, you become more efficient, confident and professional. How you feel about yourself manifests in how you handle yourself. Here are some professional tips from head to toe for men and women. The key is to implement **all** the tips, not just a few.

Your image is a "package deal" comprised of your clothing, grooming and accessories. Give yourself the competitive edge. Dress the part. How you look is crucial, so dress well and conservatively. Follow these universal tips for professional image!

Professional image is a tool that can advance your career.

Credibility Enhancers

MEN

- Conservative suit.

- Clothing tailored to body proportions. Proper fit is critical.

- Clean and neatly pressed clothes.

- Tie is clean, good quality, proper length. Pattern or colors not "distracting."

- Keep suit coat on or wear long sleeves to strengthen your authority.

- Keep jewelry simple, make sure watch is not too casual or dressy for business outfit.

- Clean shaven look is best. Facial hair should always be trimmed.

- Hair neat, clean and styled to complement face structure.

- If losing hair, let it go natural.

- Cologne, less is always better.

- Shoes, polished at all times and not worn. Watch bottoms and heels for wear. Men tend to cross the legs and the bottom of the shoes show.

- Socks same color as hemline and shoes. If in a business suit wear over-the-calf socks.

- Wallet in jacket pocket.

- Well manicured nails.

Credibility Enhancers

WOMEN

- Conservative outfit.

- Jewelry, simple, minimal and do not wear anything that jangles.

- Wear fresh, natural make-up.

- Lipstick is essential in a color which complements your natural coloring.

- Hair clean, styled to complement face structure and lifestyle with length one inch off the shoulders or above.

- Well manicured nails, one quarter inch long, polished in complementary color to your lipstick.

- Perfumes, less is always better.

- Polished, 1"-2" closed heel pump, same color or darker than hemline.

- No purse, put your wallet in briefcase. Carry a professional accessory: leather pad, appointment book or briefcase.

- Wear a coat that covers skirt or dress hemline.

- Wear a suit coat or long sleeves to create the most professional look.

- Skirt or dress length middle of the knee. (See Chapter Six.)

- Proper undergarments worn.

- Neutral color hosiery.

Credibility Enhancers

MEN AND WOMEN

- Clothes neat, clean and pressed.

- Briefcase or leather pad in neutral color and scaled to body structure.

- Gold or silver pen.

- Raincoat in neutral color and good working condition umbrella.

- Do not wear glasses that change tint with light. People need to see the eyes if they are to believe in you.

- Never wear a trendy fad or fashion.

- Clothes tailored to your body structure and height.

- Good quality materials, matched seams or patterns and well made button holes.

- Lining fabric lays neat.

Credibility Robbers

In the professional world you never want any article of clothing, grooming or accessory to take away from you. Here are the most common items professional men and women fall prey to which eliminate credibility.

MEN AND WOMEN

- Scuffed or worn shoes.

- Shoes a lighter color than hemline.

- Wearing uncomplimentary colors.

- Not having a separate work wardrobe.

- Less than 70% work attire in your closet.

- Not utilizing appearance as a positive business tool.

- Not giving thought to what level of professional dress the day dictates.

- Wearing a casual or dressy watch.

- Clothes not tailored.

- Poorly manicured nails.

- Unprofessional hairstyle.

- Wrinkled clothes.

- Scuffed or worn business accessory (leather pad, briefcase).

In the professional world you never want any article of clothing, grooming or accessory to take away from you.

- Worn or stained overcoat or raincoat.

- Umbrella is broken.

- Carrying a plastic pen.

- Dirty or slicked back hair.

- Too much cologne or perfume.

- Eyeglasses uncomplimentary in color, size or shape.

- Dark tinted glasses.

- Wearing a trendy fad or fashion.

- Briefcase not scaled to body structure and height.

Credibility Robbers

MEN

- Outdated wardrobe. Widest part of jacket lapels are not same width as widest part of the tie.

- Tie falling above or below the belt.

- Socks a different color from the shoes and hemline, or wearing no socks.

- Worn or dirty shoes.

- Facial hair in need of trimming.

- Food particles in facial hair.

- Facial hair is graying and hair on head is not, making man appear much older than he is.

- Pant length too long or short.

- Sleeve length too long or short.

- Collar pulling or gaping at the neck.

- Spotted or dirty tie.

- Collar style uncomplimentary to the shape of the face.

- Business shirt less than fifty percent cotton blend.

- Watch too casual for professional outfit.

- Individual tries to cover hair loss by pulling or brushing hair to that area.

- Material hanging or pulling in seat of the pants.

- Poor quality suit material.

- No undershirt worn under business shirt.

- Wearing bow tie.

- Wearing suspenders with a belt or with pants with belt loops.

- Clothes not tailored to body structure or height.

- Wearing unlined business jackets.

- Cannot button suit jacket without material pulling.

- Standing with double-breasted suit jacket unbuttoned.

Credibility Robbers

WOMEN

- Skirt or dress length shorter than just above the knee.

- Skirt or dress length longer than two inches below the knee.

- No make-up, too much make-up or unnatural looking make-up.

- Casual or dressy jewelry.

- Hair style inappropriate, long hair not pulled up in a professional style.

- Wearing white or cream hosiery when skirt or dress is not white or cream.

- Wearing pure black or white hosiery.

- Wearing colored tights.

- Wearing no hosiery.

- Shoe heel height is more than two inches.

- Carrying a purse.

- Shoe color lighter than hemline.

- Too much jewelry.

- Jewelry that jingles or earrings that sway when you move.

- Hair color looks unnatural.

- Wearing sleeveless tops.

- Wearing see-through materials.

- Wearing low cut blouses or dresses.

- Dress or skirt slit more than three inches.

- Wearing tennis shoes with Power Professional or Professional attire.

- Unprofessional hair accessory (e.g. rubber bands).

- Slip showing.

- Not wearing proper undergarments.

- Wearing attire too loose or too tight.

- Attire not tailored to body structure and height.

The key is to avoid **all** the listed credibility robbers. If your total image contains even one of these items, you completely defeat the purpose of creating credibility.

NOW you have your credibility checklist and understand the importance and benefits of your best professional image. Let's move into the steps of how to project your **best** appearance package through color, style of clothes, personality (textures and patterns), accessories and grooming. This is where you will learn how to save time, effort and money in establishing your wardrobe. Professionally you will gain the respect and recognition you deserve as well as see monetary gain.

Chapter Five

Color as a Business Tool

Ever have a day when people asked if you felt well? You felt just fine and were puzzled by their queries. Recall what color of attire you were wearing that day. Most likely it was a color of clothing that clashed with your natural skin undertone. Let me explain why individuals can look healthier, younger and their best while other people can look ill or older than their age just by the colors they are wearing. When you wear colors which complement your skin undertone, people remember you and not what you are wearing. You want people to remember you and not specifically what you wear.

When you wear colors which complement your skin undertone, people remember you and not what you are wearing.

As human beings we are put together to look nice. When you are born, your eye color harmonizes with your natural hair coloring and your natural skin undertone. Please note the word skin **undertone**. The undertone is the predominant color which is deep below the layers of our skin. We cannot change the skin undertone we are born with. It does not matter if our skin tans, fades, freckles or what our age or nationality is. Think about what happens when we mature. The skin lightens, the eyes fade in

*The **undertone** is the predominant color which is deep below the layers of our skin.*

We cannot change the skin undertone we are born with.

color and the hair turns gray. Everything lightens together at the same time and consequently looks nice as we age. This explains why people who change their eye color with colored contacts (for example, from brown to blue) look out of harmony and all you want to look at are their eyes. You see, they were not meant to have blue eyes. They were meant to have brown eyes. If brown-eyed people enhance their brown eyes with a brown contact or a soft green (most brown eyes have some green in them), they look nice and few people can tell they are wearing colored contacts.

We get our coloring from our grandparents, not our parents.

We get our coloring from our grandparents, not our parents. Our features come from our parents but not our coloring. That is why you can have a husband and wife with dark hair, dark eyes and medium complexion who have a blue-eyed, blonde, fair-skinned child. The child's coloring came from at least one of the four grandparents.

As children, before we go to school, we know what colors harmonize with our skin undertone, eyes and natural hair color.

Here is an interesting fact: As children, before we go to school, we know what colors harmonize with our skin undertone, eyes and natural hair color. A child of age four or five, before being influenced by fashion, peers, parents and trends will instinctively pick out what colors look best on them when you take them shopping. After five years of age we become influenced by outside forces and forget to follow our instinct. Even more interesting, when we are around sixty years old, the color instinct returns and we refuse to wear colors we do not look good in. The problem is that between five years old and sixty years old when we need to know what works best for us in color, we are too influenced by the people around us. Let's continue on to find out why this is.

People have red, yellow, blue and green hues in their skin. You are born with either blue as the predominant undertone or yellow. Everyone can wear a shade of red, yellow, blue, green and purple. For example, if you are an individual with the yellow undertone, the red you can wear will be an orange red. If you have the blue undertone, your red will be a blue red.

You are born with either blue as the predominant skin undertone or yellow.

Going through your own personal color consultation is how you learn what colors work best for you. I strongly recommend that you seek a **certified consultant**, like myself, who has had training through *Fashion Academy, Inc.* of Salt Lake City, Utah. *Gerrie Pinckney* of *Fashion Academy, Inc.* developed the following skin undertone color system. In a consultation you learn your skin undertone category. There are six skin tone categories: **Cool Violet, Cool Red, Cool Rose, Warm Golden, Warm Orange and Warm Tawny.** (See the color charts at the end of this chapter.)

Going through your own personal color consultation is how you learn what colors work best for you.

The **cool violets, cool reds** and **cool roses** have the predominant blue skin undertone. The **cool violets** have the most blue in their skin

The cool violets, cool reds and cool roses have the predominant blue skin undertone.

undertone. They look good in blue undertone colors: black, white, burgundy, blue red, purple, lemon yellow, royal blue, navy blue, blue-green teal, forest green and bright pink. Their neutral colors go very dark to medium. Their lights are like white with a splash of color in it. Their bright colors are just that—bright with a blue undertone.

The cool violets have the most blue in their skin undertone.

The **cool reds** have the blue skin undertone with some red in it. These individuals like natural colors so they try to wear brown, beige or rust but look ill in them. They need the blue undertones and should wear black, gray, taupe, burgundy, blue-green and purple. They should not wear bright colors like royal blue or bright pinks.

The cool reds have the blue skin undertone with some red in it.

The **cool roses** have a soft blue skin undertone. Interestingly, everything about them is soft including eye, skin and hair color. Often cool roses will say they have mousy looking hair color. They look best in blue undertone colors with a medium to light value and softness. For example, they look good in a soft federal blue but not a royal blue; they look good in a mauve but not a bright pink. They look excellent in medium to light soft grays, blue grays, a medium shade of navy, medium shades of burgundy or plum, soft blue-green, rosy red and pastels.

The cool roses have a soft blue skin undertone.

The **warm goldens**, **warm oranges** and **warm tawnys** have the predominant yellow skin undertone. The **warm goldens** have the most yellow undertone in their skin. They look good in yellow undertone colors that are bright and go from a medium to light value. These colors include brown, beige, peach, yellow green or teal, medium navy blue, royal blue, tomato red and brown pink. The warm goldens love their pinks. However, their warm pink is sometimes difficult to find in the stores.

The **warm oranges** have the yellow skin undertone with some red in it. They look excellent in and love the orange color family. The colors they should wear are burnt orange, rust, chocolate brown, apricot, peach, coral, golden yellow, medium navy, royal blue, a yellow-green teal, medium value purple or sage green.

The **warm tawnys** have the yellow skin undertone with a lot of red and can wear medium to darker value colors: dark brown, rust, khaki green, mustard yellow, brick red, and pea green. The colors are all soft, not bright.

The majority of the population tends to be cool violets or cool reds. There are about an even number of cool roses, warm goldens and warm oranges. There are few warm tawnys in the world.

Let me explain how we interact with each other based on our coloring and how you can use this tool to work for you in the business world. Each skin tone category tends to have certain personality traits and I believe you will agree when you read "your" description.

*The **warm goldens, warm oranges** and **warm tawnys** have the predominant yellow skin undertone.*

*The **warm goldens** have the most yellow undertone in their skin.*

*The **warm oranges** have the yellow skin undertone with some red in it.*

*The **warm tawnys** have the yellow skin undertone with a lot of red.*

Cool violets and **cool reds** have a lot of color contrast between their hair, skin and eyes. They usually have darker hair. They tend to be very independent, outgoing and give the appearance they can handle everything. The truth is they are very sensitive and wish others would recognize that. Cool violets and cool reds create a sense of authority, an "I mean business" facade, and oftentimes appear to be mad but are not. They will appear not to be listening to you yet they are hanging on your every word. They want to know it all. If you ask cool violets or cool reds about something and they do not know, they will say they do and then will go find out the answer. Cool violets and cool reds tend to be leaders and have no problem talking with others.

Cool violets and cool reds tend to be independent, outgoing and give the appearance they can handle everything.

Cool violets and cool reds can be intimidating even before they speak, due to their color contrast. This is how they can use color to their advantage. To create a sense of authority, cool violets and cool reds wear black, gray, navy, dark burgundy, dark plum, dark purple colors. To create approachability, wear medium to bright colors: taupe, royal blue, teal green, light blue, blue-green, and pink.

The **cool roses** are very "soft" and are perceived this way from birth. This is because their hair, skin and eyes are very soft in appearance. They tend to grow up being very laid back. The world could be crashing around them and they would be saying, "It's okay, everything will work out." They prefer not being in the spotlight.

Cool roses prefer not being in the spotlight.

Cool roses may appear to have a difficult time making decisions because they are more analytical than spontaneous and want to make the "right" decision. They are excellent workers on their own; give them a job and they will pay attention to details and do excellent work. Cool roses are not lengthy talkers unless you really get to know them. They are good hearted people and will give you "the shirt off their back." Cool roses age very gracefully because the skin, eyes and hair are already lighter or softer in appearance. They are very approachable, never intimidating. To create authority, cool roses need to wear charcoal gray, medium navy, medium burgundy and plum colors. They are approachable in soft blue, soft pink, rose, and soft green.

The **warm goldens** and **warm oranges** are very friendly people. They tend to smile a lot and when they smile their eyes twinkle. This is why they age around the eyes first. Warm goldens and warm oranges age gracefully. They typically have light to medium skin with light to medium blue or brown eyes and light to medium blonde or brown hair. Never underestimate their intelligence; they like to learn and know a great deal. They are not intimidating but are very approachable people. To create authority, they need to wear medium brown or medium navy. Their approachability

Warm goldens and warm oranges are very friendly people.

colors: royal blue, teal, coral, beige, tomato red, banana yellow, peach or warm pink.

The **warm tawny** is a combination of the cool violet and warm golden traits. Warm tawnys tend to be outgoing and friendly at the same time. They have a tendency to appear to be disorganized but they know what they are doing every minute. They also tend to be intimidating with their appearance so they should wear orange, teal and purple to create approachability. To create authority, dark brown, rust or deep sage green work best.

Refer to the charts to determine what works best for each color category. Note you only need two pairs of shoes, two belts and one color hosiery to go with everything in your wardrobe. (For women: only three shades of lipsticks.)

Naturally, you can have more items but you only need the above numbers. For example: Shoe color should be the same color or darker than your hemline. We look at people from their feet to their face. We want people to focus on the face. The face is where your personality and qualities are expressed. If your shoes are inappropriately lighter than the hemline, we tend to look at the feet and never get to the face. This is an example where you do NOT want to follow fashion fads in your professional wardrobe. You want people to remember you and not your shoes.

*The **warm tawny** is outgoing and friendly.*

Shoe color should be the same color or darker than your hemline.

We look at people from their feet to their face.

The color charts on the following pages will show the neutral colors, bright colors and light colors for each skin undertone color category. The neutral colors are best for business suits and pants. Light colors are best for men's shirts, women's blouses, dresses and summer suits. The bright colors are best for men's ties, casual clothes, women's blouses, suits, dresses, skirts and pants.

Cool Violet Color Chart

Neutral colors:

Black, charcoal gray, medium gray, light gray, medium to light blue gray, taupe*, medium to light taupe, dark navy, medium to light blue

* Taupe has gray in it so it looks gray, not tan.

Light colors:

Ice blue, ice pink, ice green, ice yellow, ice violet, ice aqua, ice periwinkle, white, cream

Ice is white with just a touch of color.

Bright colors:

Royal blue, teal blue, blue violet, fuschia pink, turquoise, blue-green, burgundy, maroon, blue red, garnet red, ruby red, indigo, plum, purple, lemon yellow

Shoes and belts:

Men: black and burgundy
Women: black and navy

Hosiery:

Men: black, dark gray, navy
Women: nude, taupe, navy, soft black

Cool Red Color Chart

Neutral colors:

Black, charcoal gray, medium gray, light gray, medium to light blue gray, taupe*, medium to light taupe, dark navy, medium to light blue, mahogany is so dark it looks black.

* Taupe has gray in it so it looks gray not tan.

Light colors:

Medium to light sky blue, yellow, periwinkle, aqua, pink, rose, mint green, white, cream

Bright colors:

These colors are medium to darker shades. Blue violet, purple, royal blue, azure blue, plum red, burgundy, red rose, indigo, plum, cranberry, canary yellow, pine green, spruce green, turquoise, eucalyptus green

Shoes and belts:

Men: black and cordovan (burgundy)
Women: black and burgundy or gray

Hosiery:

Men: black, gray, navy
Women: nude, taupe, gray, navy, soft black

Cool Rose Color Chart

Neutral colors:

Charcoal gray, medium gray, light gray, medium to light gray blue, navy medium to light, blue gray medium to light, medium to light rose brown

Light colors:

Medium to light pastels of baby blue, periwinkle, aqua, pink, rose, mauve, mint green or soft yellow, off-white, cream

Bright colors:

These colors are medium shades and are soft in appearance. Blue violet, purple, cadet blue, delft or sky blue, aquamarine blue, plum red, burgundy, red rose, raspberry, indigo, violet, wine, mulberry, plum grape, butter yellow, jade, spruce green, turquoise, blue teal

Shoes and belts:

Men: black and cordovan (burgundy)
Women: burgundy or navy and gray

Hosiery:

Men: black, gray, navy
Women: nude, taupe, soft navy, gray

Warm Golden Color Chart

Neutral colors:

Dove gray, medium gray, light gray, medium to light navy, medium to light royal blue, medium brown to light brown, camel, tan, bronze to a light cream beige

Light colors:

Medium to light tints of sky blue, periwinkle, aqua, pink-coral, coral, mint green, violet, peach, ivory

Bright colors:

These colors are medium shades. Purple, royal blue, azure blue, violet, daisy yellow, daffodil yellow, kelly green, apple green, turquoise, lettuce green, coral, tomato red, mandarin red, pink-coral

Shoes and belts:

Men: black and brown
Women: brown and navy

Hosiery:

Men: black, dark brown, navy
Women: nude, suntan, beige, soft navy

Warm Orange Color Chart

Neutral colors:

Medium gray to light gray, medium to light navy, medium sable brown to light warm beige, red brown, rust brown to a light terra cotta

Light colors:

Medium to light tints of blue, periwinkle, aqua, teal, terra cotta, peach, tan, maize, sage green, cream

Bright colors:

These colors are medium to darker shades. Violet, peacock blue, teal blue, brick red, turquoise, avocado green, olive green, pea green, apricot, autumn gold, corn yellow, tangerine orange, copper, terra cotta, hot pepper red

Shoes and belts:

Men: black and dark brown
Women: brown and navy

Hosiery:

Men: black, dark brown, navy
Women: nude, suntan, beige, soft navy

Warm Tawny Color Chart

Neutral colors:

Smoky gray, medium gray, light gray, medium to light blue, dark brown to light beige, bronze, tan to cream

Light colors:

Soft medium to light tints of blue, periwinkle, aqua, peach, mustard yellow, sage, tan, terra cotta, beige

Bright colors:

These colors are soft medium to darker shades. Violet, purple, teal blue, sunflower yellow, sage green, olive green, turquoise, moss green, burnt orange, gold, brick red, brown red

Shoes and belts:

Men: black and dark brown
Women: brown and rust brown

Hosiery:

Men: black, dark brown
Women: nude, beige, cinnamon

Benefits of Color
Professionally & Personally

You can use color to work beneficially as a tool in your job and save thousands of dollars in your wardrobe.

You can use color to work beneficially as a tool in your job and save thousands of dollars in your wardrobe.

Professional Benefits

1) Wear your neutral colors, which tend to be your darker colors, to create authority. When you need others to take you seriously or are in a presentation situation, wear your dark neutral colors.

2) White or cream colored shirts or blouses with your neutral colors create authority, credibility, and respect.

3) To create approachability, your basic and light colors work best.

4) We look at people from their feet to their face. If you wear **only** colors which enhance you, people immediately remember you and not what you were wearing.

5) You will look healthier.

Personal Benefits

1) You will save time shopping in stores by only looking at colors which enhance you.

2) You only need two different color pairs of shoes to go with everything in your wardrobe.*

3) You only need two colors of belts to go with everything in your wardrobe.*

4) A woman only needs three shades of lipstick and one color of foundation.*

5) Coordinating your attire for the day becomes effortless.

6) You can have fewer clothes in your closet if you filter out of your wardrobe what does not work best for you and bring in only those colors that do enhance you.

7) When you shop and bring an article of clothing home not only will it go with the outfit you had in mind, you will find it will go with many pieces of attire in your closet.

* Note: You can have more shoes, belts, and lipsticks but you only need the number mentioned above.

Chapter Six

Look Good and Feel Good in Your Best Styles

How the Fit of Your Attire Affects Your Professionalism

Just as you are born with your coloring, as explained in the chapter on color, you are also born with your bone structure. You cannot change your bone structure which means the styles of clothing that work for you **always** will and the styles of clothing which do not work for you **never** will. If fashion brings out a style that does NOT complement your body structure, do NOT buy it! People will not remember if you were in fashion, they will remember if you look nice. It does not matter if you gain weight, lose weight or tone your muscle tissue, the styles that complement your body structure always will.

The shape of your face determines which hairstyles, collars and accessories are most flattering. The shoulder shape determines whether you need shoulder pads and what kind. The shoulder shape also determines collar types and sleeve seam types most appropriate for you.

When clothing styles complement your body structure, you appear professional.

The hip type determines the styles of tops, shirts, blouses, suits, dresses, pants and jackets that will look best. The bone structure, combined with your height, determines the style of attire, size of patterns, length of sleeves and hemlines that work best.

Let's learn what your body structure consists of so you have a clear understanding of what styles of clothing work best for you. When clothing styles complement your body structure, you appear professional. Clothing which does not enhance your body structure will appear sloppy and not fine-tuned. A fine-tuned appearance represents professionalism to employers and customers. If men and women take the time with their appearance they will pay attention to details in their job.

FACE

The shape of the face determines which hairstyles, collars and accessories are the most flattering.

There are nine face shapes: oval, round, square, rectangular, oblong, heart, triangle, inverted triangle and diamond. When you get out of the shower or bath, brush your hair straight back. Look in the mirror and determine which face shape you have.

Men have five different collar styles: round, regular, pinned-down, button-down and spread. A round, inverted triangle or square face shape should wear the regular, pinned down or button down collar. An oval face shape can wear any of the collar styles. An oblong, rectangular, triangle, diamond face shape should wear the regular, round or spread collar style.

Women's tops, blouses and dresses will have a v-neck, scoop, shawl or square collar style. The round face shape should wear the v-neck, deep scoop, shawl or square collar style. The oval face shape can wear any collar style. The square face shape looks best in a v-neck, scoop or shawl collar. The oblong, rectangular, triangle, heart and diamond face shapes look best in a shorter v-neck, square or high cut scoop neckline.

SHOULDERS

Shoulders determine the appropriate lapel style in jackets. Lapel styles are peaked, semi-peaked, standard or shawl. Men and women have very squared, slightly squared, tapered or sloped shoulders.

Shoulders determine the appropriate lapel style in jackets.

Men and women with squared or slightly squared shoulders look best in a standard notched lapel or shawl collar. Men and women with tapered shoulders look best in standard or semi-peaked lapels. Men and women with sloped shoulders look best in standard, semi-peaked or peaked lapels.

HIPS

Hips determine the style of shirt, jacket and pants for a man and the style of blouse, jacket, pants, skirt and dress for a woman. There are three different hip types: high hip, tapered hip and in between hip. Very few people in the population have an in between hip, most will have either a high hip or tapered hip.

Hip type
determines
the style of
shirt, jacket
and pants for
the man and
the style of
blouse, jacket,
pants, skirt
and dress for
a woman.

The high hip is determined by feeling with your hand where your hip bone is located. The high hip man or woman will carry their body weight in the upper half of the body. If you ask them about their waist they will say, "What waist?" The chest and stomach area is full and if this individual lost every pound but one, it would remain in the stomach. Their plus is they have flat buttocks and slim thighs compared to the tapered hip.

The tapered hip man and woman will find their hip bones sit closer to the ground. For this reason this man or woman carries weight in the buttocks and upper thighs. If they lost every pound but one, it would remain in the buttocks and upper thighs. Their plus is they have a medium to slim waist.

Men have three jacket styles: European, American or Natural cut. The European is a more fitted jacket. The American is fuller through the chest area and is semi-fitted. The Natural cut is a fuller jacket. Men have options of the one, two, three, four button jacket or double breasted jacket. Jacket pockets may be inset, flap, patch or double flap. The two most common pockets are the inset and flap. Jackets have a rear center vent, double vent or no vent.

Men's pants may be pleated, plain top pants, cuffed, straight, flared or tapered. Men's pants have side seam or slant pockets. Men's shirts are fitted or unfitted. The man's tie is offered in three different lengths corresponding to height: short, medium or tall. Men, the tip of your tie should hit the middle of your belt buckle or waistband.

The double breasted suit is made only for the tall man (over 6'0") or tall woman (over 5'9") with a small bone structure. These individuals appear to be very slender and have the height to carry the double breasted suit. The double breasted suit has a straight hem which cuts off height and makes a person appear shorter. For this reason the short or medium height individual looks shorter in this style. The double breasted suit always comes with cuffed pants. Cuffed pants also make a person look shorter. Naturally, a tall person can afford to wear the cuffed pants while the short or medium height person will look shorter. A double breasted suit wraps extra material across the waist. If you carry your weight in the stomach or chest area, now you appear to be heavier. If you are medium build, now you are covering up your best asset. **Note:** The double breasted suit is meant always to be buttoned when standing.

For the tapered hip man, here are your best shirt, jacket and pant styles. The best jacket styles are the European and American cut

The double breasted suit is made only for the tall man (over 6'0") or tall woman (over 5'9") with a small bone structure.

The double breasted suit is meant always to be buttoned when standing.

because they are fitted or semi-fitted to complement your waist. The center vent jacket will work best for the tapered hip man.

If you carry a lot of weight in your buttocks and thighs, wear the double vent to give you more room. A regular or semi-fitted shirt works best for you. Your best pants are pleated, straight leg pants with inset pockets.

For the high hip man the American and Natural cut jackets with the center vent or no vent and flap pockets work best. The regular shirt gives you the room you need. Pants should have a single pleat or no pleat. The high hip man should wear the tapered pants leg.

The hemline of the jacket should always cover the buttocks.

The hemline of the jacket should always cover the buttocks. The upper back of a man's suit should lay flat and not buckle up. One way you can tell if a man is updated in his attire is if the widest part of the jacket lapel is the same width as the widest part of the tie. A man's shirt collar should be one half inch above the jacket collar in the back. If the shirt collar is too tight, it is time to purchase a shirt in a half size larger. If you wear long sleeves with your suit coats and sport coats, the shirt sleeve length should be one half inch below the wrist bone and the coat length should be right at the wrist bone.

Have your clothes tailored.

Note: Have your clothes tailored. The tailor should measure both arms and both legs since every man and woman has one arm and leg longer than the other. Wear the shoes you will wear with these clothes. When you pick up your tailoring, put the clothes back on with the proper shoes and check each arm and each leg for the proper length. If they are not comfortable or are the wrong length, have them re-done; otherwise, you will never look professional or feel your best in those clothes.

Pants should have a slight crease in the front. Too much of a crease means they are too long and no crease means they are too short. The front pant hem should rest slightly on the top of your shoe. The back of the pant hem should hit the middle of the back of the shoe.

Women with a high hip, the best blouses are the ones made to wear outside of your pants or skirts. If you tuck a blouse in, pull it out a little. The best length for tops, sweaters or suit jackets is just below the bottom of the hip bone. A straight or semi-fitted jacket will complement your upper body. A peplum style jacket works wonderfully because it will give you the illusion of having a waist and this type of suit always comes with a straight skirt. The best skirt has no waist band, darts or tucks. A straight or pleated skirt or dress looks very complementary to your body structure. The best skirt or dress hem length is middle of the knee or one to two inches above the knee. **Note:** Measure from the middle of the knee. A hemline shorter than this becomes unprofessional and is not

The tailor should measure both arms and both legs since every man and woman has one arm and leg longer than the other.

When you pick up your tailoring, put the clothes back on with the proper shoes and check each arm and each leg for the proper length.

The best skirt or dress hem length is middle of the knee.

appropriate for the work situation. A straight or semi-fitted dress with no belt is a good choice. Many times you can just remove the belt and belt loops and the dress will work fine for you. Clothing manufacturers often make your dress style but tend to put a belt with it.

A slant pocket can be worn in your skirts, dresses and pants. Your best pants are tapered pants with no waist-band or belt. You look great in stirrup pants, but do not wear them to work because they are not professional pants. Stirrup pants are a casual pant for outside of work. Even if the company is business casual, do not wear stirrup pants.

The tapered hip woman looks best with tops and blouses tucked in. Dresses and pants should have a belt. The best belt width is one to two inches. A wider belt covers up your best feature, your waist. Skirts and pants need darts, tucks or pleats at the waistband.

An a-line skirt or dress is very becoming on your body structure. The best hem length for your skirt or dress is middle of the knee or one to two inches past the middle of your knee. If the hemline goes longer, the outfit now becomes business casual.

The best jacket is the semi- or fitted with the hemline just below your buttocks and not shorter. The jacket length can go longer if you are 5'7" or taller. The inset pocket works best on your jackets.

The sleeve for a woman is the same as the man. A long sleeve blouse should be one half inch past your wrist bone and the jacket sleeve should hit right at the wrist bone. If you tend to wear short sleeve blouses under your jackets, the jacket sleeve needs to be one half inch past the wrist bone.

Shoulder pads are available to balance out the shoulders with the hips. The squared shoulder woman does NOT need shoulder pads. The woman with the slightly squared shoulders can go without shoulder pads or wear the rounded shoulder pads. The tapered and sloped shouldered woman should wear the squared shoulder pads.

Shoulder pads balance out the shoulders with the hips for most women.

Purchase a pair of shoulder pads from the local fabric store. Buy shoulder pads that can be placed on the shoulders, need no attachment and will not slip. Check the shoulder pads in the clothes you are purchasing, since many times they are the wrong shoulder pads. Remove them and replace with your correct shoulder pads.

Straight leg pants with darts, tucks, or pleats at the waistband work best for the tapered hip woman. The darts, tucks or pleats give the added room needed through the buttocks and thighs. Side seam pockets work best on your pants, skirts and dresses as opposed to slant pockets.

Cuffed pants are for the tall woman 5'7" and above. Cuffed pants will make your legs appear shorter.

Have your clothes tailored.

The double breasted suit is only complementary to the tall, small boned woman or man.

Note: Have your clothes tailored. The tailor should measure both arms and both legs since every man and woman has one arm and leg longer than the other. Wear the shoes you will wear with these clothes. When you pick up your tailoring, put the clothes back on with the proper shoes and check each arm and each leg for the proper length. If the clothes are not comfortable or are the wrong length, have them re-done; otherwise, you will never look professional or feel your best in those clothes.

The tailor should measure both arms and both legs since every man and woman has one arm and leg longer than the other.

Professional Benefits of a Proper Fit

- Proper sleeve lengths give a neat professional appearance.

- Tailored clothing sends a professional message as opposed to clothing that fits too big or too tight.

- Clothing properly tailored to your body structure makes you feel comfortable.

- When clothes are tailored, you can concentrate on what you have to do that day and not on what you are wearing.

Chapter Seven

Be Professional and Be Your Own Person

Personality "Being Authentically You"

We assume that to look our professional best we have to wear clothes we do not like, wear what is in fashion or spend a lot of money. All of these assumptions are wrong. To look your professional best is about being authentically you through your wardrobe, grooming and accessories. Two people can project a different image yet both project a professional image.

To look your professional best is about being authentically you through your wardrobe, grooming and accessories.

You know when you feel comfortable in your clothes and with your appearance and others can tell as well. Learning what works best for you as an individual allows you to be comfortable and present **your professional best**!

You represent your personality through the textures, patterns, accessories and hairstyles you choose.

By following the professional image check-list and understanding your personality in dress, you will feel and look your best. Here is a test to help you understand what personality you are.

Lifestyle influences your image at work, home and socially. This test will answer why you love an article of clothing in your closet and why other pieces of clothing just hang in the closet year to year. Once you know the **why,** you eliminate ever having items of clothing that you do not wear. Yes, you will see a tremendous money savings in your wardrobe.

Authentically You

Your personal style

*Check all the words which describe
your personality.*

❶
- ☐ Aggressive
- ☐ Distant
- ☐ Daring
- ☐ In vogue
- ☐ Sophisticated
- ☐ Self-assured
- ☐ Confident
- ☐ Intense
- ☐ Capable
- ☐ Demanding

❷
- ☐ Conservative
- ☐ Poised
- ☐ Courteous
- ☐ Refined
- ☐ Reserved
- ☐ Stately
- ☐ Serene
- ☐ Meticulous
- ☐ Proficient
- ☐ Dignified

*Add up the number
of boxes in each
column and record.*

❶ *Dramatic* _____

❷ *Classic* _____

❸ *Natural* _____

❹ *Romantic* _____

❸
- ☐ Casual
- ☐ Cheerful
- ☐ Energetic
- ☐ Enthusiastic
- ☐ Friendly
- ☐ Optimistic
- ☐ Spontaneous
- ☐ Nonconformist
- ☐ Independent
- ☐ Adventuresome

❹
- ☐ Glamorous
- ☐ Flirtatious
- ☐ Daring
- ☐ Exciting
- ☐ Provocative
- ☐ Soft
- ☐ Charming
- ☐ Elegant
- ☐ Very feminine
- ☐ Softly sophisticated

Lifestyle

Check the events which you will attend on a regular basis this year.

☐ Ballet	☐ Craft fairs
☐ Spectator sports	☐ Fund-raisers
☐ Museums	☐ Church events
☐ Theater	☐ PTA meetings
❶ ☐ Concerts	❷ ☐ Political functions
☐ Premiers	☐ Community
☐ Night life	☐ Volunteering
☐ Opening nights	☐ School activities
☐ Formal parties	☐ Formal dining
☐ Fashion shows	☐ Cultural events

Add up the number of boxes in each column and record.

❶ *Dramatic* _____

❷ *Classic* _____

❸ *Natural* _____

❹ *Romantic* _____

☐ Sports	☐ Lunch/friends
☐ Gardening	☐ Garden parties
☐ Hobbies	☐ Inside activities
☐ Spectator sports	☐ Resort vacations
❸ ☐ Outdoor activities	❹ ☐ Patio entertaining
☐ Informal parties	☐ Dressy parties
☐ Travel	☐ Dancing
☐ Exercise	☐ Night life
☐ Camping	☐ Opera
☐ Sightseeing	☐ Music reviews

Your Preferences

Check one answer per question.

1. What are your favorite colors?
   A. contrasting—black/white or bold and strong
   B. neutrals, pastels
   C. medium to dark earthy tones
   D. bright, clear, jewel tones

2. What are your favorite fabrics:
   A. leather, flannel, silk
   B. soft wool, cashmere, rayon, suede, silk
   C. cotton, denim, tweed, ribbed knit, gauze
   D. silk, chiffon, knit, lightweight

3. Which hairstyle do you prefer?
   A. striking, sculpted, angled
   B. controlled, conservative
   C. casual, care free, minimal care
   D. soft, longer

4. What is your preferred day outfit?
   A. unconventional separates
   B. tailored separates
   C. jeans or comfortable separates
   D. soft separates

5. What do you want most next year?
   A. recognition, status
   B. family, home
   C. fun, friends
   D. attention, self-expression

6. How do you like your clothes to fit?
   A. controlled, structured
   B. tailored
   C. loose, comfortable
   D. body conforming, loose/tight combined

7. What is your favorite accessory?
   A. sunglasses
   B. nice gold or silver watch
   C. leather band watch
   D. jeweled rings

Add up your A, B, C, D responses and record.

Ⓐ *Dramatic* _____

Ⓑ *Classic*   _____

Ⓒ *Natural*   _____

Ⓓ *Romantic* _____

Courtesy of Fashion Academy, Inc.

Now total all the numbers in Dramatic, Classic, Natural and Romantic from all three sections and record here.

_____   Dramatic

_____   Classic

_____   Natural

_____   Romantic

Read on to understand how this relates to the textures, patterns, accessories and hairstyles you choose. Note: Your lifestyle may dictate you to dress one way yet you would like to dress differently. For example: You may want to be more classic but you have children you are driving to sporting events. This lifestyle dictates you to be more natural. Another example: You would like to be more natural at work but you are in a very visible position so your job prescribes a more classic appearance.

Dramatic

Body type:	*angular, slender*
Facial features:	*defined, angular*
Hair:	*severe, sleek, wild*
Patterns:	*geometric, bold, exotic*
Textures:	*suede, leather, silk*
Accessories:	*large, bold, heavy*

Natural

Body type:	*average to tall, athletic*
Facial features:	*long, broad, square*
Hair:	*windblown, carefree, casual*
Patterns:	*solid, plaid*
Textures:	*tweed, corduroy, denim, knit*
Accessories:	*plain, leather band watch, little or no jewelry*

Classic

Body type:	*average balanced body structure*
Facial features:	*even or rounded*
Hairstyle:	*simple, soft, neat, controlled*
Patterns:	*solid, paisley, traditional or curved*
Textures:	*silk, smooth, plain texture*
Accessories:	*controlled, modest, curved*

Romantic

Body type:	*rounded or tall slender*
Facial features:	*round, soft, youthful*
Hairstyle:	*soft curls, waves, feathered*
Patterns:	*flowered print, curved*
Textures:	*soft materials, silk*
Accessories:	*small, dainty, intricate*

Benefits of Being
Authentically You Professionally

1) In business others can tell if you are comfortable with your appearance. By representing **your** personality through the patterns and textures of materials, hairstyles and jewelry, you will feel comfortable and, thus, others with you. The key is to stay within the personality guideline which was discussed in the chapter on **Personality**.

2) You will save yourself money by not purchasing what is currently in fashion (pattern, texture, hairstyles, jewelry) if it does not represent your personality. People do not remember if you are in fashion, but they do remember if you look professional.

   There is a difference between being in fashion or being outdated in your appearance. Refer to the chapter on **Credibility Enhancers and Credibility Robbers**.

3) Personality is the reason you have so many clothes in your closet you do not wear. Once you have filtered out those articles of clothing and bring in the clothes you are comfortable in, you will save yourself time and effort in getting dressed each day.

Chapter Eight

Importance of Fine Details: Accessories

This chapter will explain how to choose accessories to enhance your personality and project your **best** professional image.

Shoes

Naturals:	textured leather
Classics:	smooth leather
Romantics:	smooth or shiny leather
	Men like the tassel, women
	like bows.
Dramatics:	smooth leather with design

Only two pairs of shoes are needed because your shoe color should be the same color or darker than your hemline.

Cool Violet/Cool Red:

Women and men: black/burgundy

Cool Rose:

Women: navy/gray   Men: black/gray

Warm Golden/Warm Orange:

Women: navy/brown   Men: black/brown

Warm Tawny:

Women: rust/brown   Men: black/brown

A one to two inch heel on a closed-in pump is the most professional shoe for a woman. A flat slip-on or tie shoe is for casual wear. Higher than a two-inch pump becomes evening wear. Men, a slip-on or tie shoe with a plain or wing tip toe with a thin or thick leather or rubber sole is for professional wear. A penny loafer shoe is casual.

Professional Accessory

Make sure the size of your briefcase or appointment book complements your height and bone structure. For example, a short man or woman should not carry a large, four-inch wide briefcase. A complementary choice would be a two-inch wide briefcase. Naturals prefer an accessory with texture or hard leathers. Classics, Romantics and Dramatics will prefer the soft leather and smooth texture.

Cool Violet/Cool Red: black, burgundy, navy, gray or taupe (choose taupe with gray in it, not beige or tan).

Cool Rose: burgundy, navy or gray

Warm Golden/Warm Orange: brown, tan, navy

Warm Tawny: dark brown, tan, olive

Watch

Naturals: prefer a leather band

Cools: choose a black or burgundy band

Warms: choose a brown or tan band

Classics: prefer a smooth metal band

Romantics: like gems in the watch with a metal band or an intricate design

Dramatics: prefer large or chunky metal banded watches

Cools look best in silver or pewter accessories. Warms look best in gold or bronze accessories.

Pen

Carry a **good quality** silver, gold or colored pen as opposed to a plastic pen. Follow the color choices from above.

Earrings

Women: Keep the size of the earrings in proportion to the size of your bone structure and height.

Short height: small to medium size

Average height: medium size

Tall height: medium to large size

Do not wear earrings that sway when you move. The earrings will become a distraction and will take away from the message you are trying to communicate. Men: Wearing no earring(s) is still the most professional. However, it is becoming more acceptable for a man to wear a small diamond or post earring in one ear.

Before doing so, check with the company to see if wearing an earring(s) is acceptable for your industry and position. Keeping your accessories simple is always key to a professional appearance.

Necklaces

For both men and women, the most complementary length of your necklace depends on the shape of your face. If you have a round or square face, then a mid to longer length necklace will work best. If you have an oblong, rectangular, heart or triangular shaped face, the mid to shorter length works best. This also applies to collar lengths for women.

Bracelets

Do not wear anything that jingles or jangles. Keep bracelets simple.

Naturals: like little jewelry.

Classics: will wear one bracelet on each arm.

Romantics: like to wear many pieces of jewelry. Do not wear more than two bracelets on each wrist and two necklaces for work.

Dramatics: could go crazy with accessories so tone down and wear fewer. No more than two bracelets on each wrist and two rings on each hand is appropriate. If you are in a financial or personal business, one bracelet on each wrist and one ring on each hand is more appropriate.

Pins, Cuff links, Tie tacks...

For women, pins are a nice way to represent personality. Naturals can complete their look with a pin since they do not care for a lot of jewelry. Most natural men do not prefer cuff links. It is the romantic or dramatic man who likes to wear cuff links and tie tacks.

Hair Accessories

An area women neglect is the hair accessory. The hair accessory can represent your personality and should be of good quality. Stay away from pony tail holders, rubber bands or bobby pins for work.

Rings

One ring per hand is the most professional.

Grooming

Women: complementary colored nail polish and natural looking make up.

Eyeglasses

Many men and women wear glasses. Eyeglasses are a very visual accessory. Eyeglasses are an investment in your eyes and appearance. When purchasing eyeglasses look for these three things.

One: The color should be complementary to you. See the color choices from your color chart in the chapter on color. Cools look best in silver (brushed or shiny) and pewter metal. Warms look best in the gold, bronze and copper metals.

Two: The size of the frames need to be in proportion to your body structure and height. A small man or woman should select a small frame, a medium man or woman a medium frame and a larger man or woman a larger frame. Most frames come in one to three different sizes. Be sure to ask if the frame you like comes in other sizes.

Three: The shape of the frame needs to enhance your face shape. A round face shape needs a squared or partly square frame. A square face shape needs a round or partly curved frame. An oblong shaped face does not want a frame that appears oblong just as the rectangular shaped face does not want a frame that is square or rectangular. Triangular or heart shaped faces need to stay away from frames that are wider at the top and narrower at the bottom.

The oval shaped face can choose any shape of frame, just watch the size and color of the frame.

Men have more choices with the bridge of the glasses than women do. When choosing glasses, if you have a longer nose, choose a bridge that drops lower on the nose or a double bridge.

For a shorter nose go with a high bridge. (Note: Most women's glasses do not have double bridges.) If you do not wear contact lenses and cannot see with your glasses off, take a trained image consultant with you to pick out your glasses. Stay away from tinted glasses because they tend to make it difficult for others to see your eyes. People feel uncomfortable when they cannot see your eyes. Accessories are the fine details of completing the appearance package.

Most men and women have difficulty looking complete in their appearance package. Here is an easy way to know if you are complete before you leave home. You receive a point for each accessory you have on, a point for each article of clothing and additional points for each new color or design. **The goal is to have fourteen points.** IF you are below fourteen points, do NOT change the whole outfit, only change a tie for a man and a blouse or an accessory for the woman. If you have between fourteen and twenty-four points, that is fine. If you have more than twenty-four points, then remove an accessory or replace an article of clothing with less color or pattern in it.

Follow these rules for simplicity in coordinating patterns and accessories. If the outfit has a lot of pattern, you want to accessorize less. If the outfit has little to no pattern you can accessorize more.

14 Point Finishing Look

Shoes:

Begin with two points, one for each shoe

Add one point for each: Contrasting stitching, ornamentation, each new color

Hosiery:

Women: One point for any color but flesh tone

Men: One point for each sock and an additional point for patterned socks

Garment:

One point for each:

New color

Contrasting buttons, belt

Pattern or design

Pocket (s)

Tie: add points for new colors

Jewelry:

One point for each:

Watch

Each ring

Each bracelet

Each necklace

Hair ornament

Each set of earrings

Cufflinks or tie clip/tack

Monogram

Eyeglasses:

Add an additional point for new colors

Accessories:

Point for each briefcase, appointment book, raincoat or hat

Goal: To have fourteen to twenty four points.

Benefits of Fine Details:
Accessories

1) When you pay attention to your accessories it projects to others that you will pay attention to details in your job.

2) Accessories complete your appearance package.

3) An accessory can make or break the image you project.

4) Neat, clean accessories send the message you care about the image you project.

Chapter Nine

Grooming for the Professional Man

Personal hygiene is important in the care of our bodies and the image we project. Bathing or showering everyday should be standard practice along with regular doctor and dentist visits, eating and exercising properly. Drink plenty of water. Water helps moisturize and purify the skin. Water also helps us maintain or lose weight.

Water helps moisturize and purify the skin— it also helps us maintain or lose weight.

Skin care

Skin care is important for a man. A man normally stays younger looking longer because he shaves the dead cells from his face and exercises the muscles in his face when he shaves. Use a moisturizer on your face and all over your body. The skin dehydrates with age and a moisturizer slows that part of the aging process.

A skin care step men need to follow is to use an exfoliant like a scrub to deep cleanse the skin. A deep cleanser gets to the second and third layer of the skin that soap does not. If your skin type is **normal**, use the deep cleanser once a week. If your skin type is **oily**, use the deep cleanser no more than twice a week. If

The shape of a man's face will determine if he looks good in a beard, mustache or beard-mustache combination.

you use a deep cleanser too often, you activate the oil glands and find yourself needing to cleanse more. If this is the case, only use a scrub twice a week and the oil glands will eventually slow down. For skin that is **dry**, deep cleanse one to two times a month. Scrubs are good for preventing blemishes.

Facial hair

The clean shaven look is the most professional look. The shape of a man's face will determine if he looks good in a beard, mustache or beard-mustache combination. Some men can carry the look of facial hair but many cannot. If you have facial hair, it is important to make sure it is trimmed and clean every day. Beware of food particles clinging to your facial hair. Always visit the bathroom after eating to check facial hair for food particles. Otherwise, it could lead to a very embarrassing situation. Men age first in the facial hair while the hair on the head is still not gray. Either color your facial hair or shave off the facial hair; otherwise, you will appear older than your years.

Balding

If you are losing hair, let it go naturally. Your hair grows in a particular pattern and if you try to comb your hair against the grain of growth, it looks ridiculous. For example, if hair loss is from the temples back and you have always combed your hair back, do not decide to

If you are losing hair, let it go naturally.

start combing your hair to the side. Unless you can afford a natural looking hair piece, do not attempt cheap imitations. It becomes necessary to keep your hair cut shorter if you are balding. What often happens to men who lose hair on their head is that hair starts growing out of their nose or ears. Nose or ear hair can be removed with tweezers.

Hair styles

Hair styled so the length does not touch a man's collar is the most professional. Depending on a man's profession, type of industry, position and shape of face, a slightly longer length may work. The shape of the face determines the style that looks best. **Round** faces look better with their hair parted on the side and combed back. The bowl cut does not work on a round face. A **square** face needs some softness by brushing the hair back and not going with an angular or blunt cut. An **oval** shaped face has no style restrictions. **Oblong and rectangular** shaped faces can go slightly longer with their hair to offset the length of their face. It is important to communicate this information to your stylist to receive the style and cut that works best for you.

The shape of the face determines the style that looks best.

Hair color needs to appear natural. If you choose to color your hair or facial hair, no one but yourself should be able to tell when it is time to color your hair again. Cosmetologists usually have no training to be able to look at you and determine your skin undertone. Communicate this information to your stylist to receive the correct hair color.

Cools: Mixing blue and violet is the key in hair color; blonde shades need to be an ash blonde (ash has gray in it).

Warms: Mixing gold and orange is the key in hair color; blonde shades need to be a golden blonde (golden has beige in it), red shades need to be an orange or strawberry red.

The following checklist will help you communicate to your stylist your ability to work with your hair, the texture of your hair, the shape of your face along with your personality.

Personality:

☐ **Natural** you do not want to fuss with your hair, you want a wash and wear hair style.

☐ **Classic** you will use the blow dryer and it is important for your hair to look styled and controlled.

☐ **Romantic** you will fuss with your hair and like the soft look.

☐ **Dramatic** you like to experiment with your hair and like the angular look.

Ability to work with your hair:

☐ excellent ☐ good ☐ fair ☐ poor

Texture of your hair:

☐ thick   ☐ thin   ☐ course   ☐ fine

Shape of your face:

☐ round

☐ square

☐ oblong or rectangular

☐ heart or triangular

☐ oval

Round you need your hair styled back away from your face.

Square you need softness and curves styled in your hair.

Oblong or rectangular you need some fullness on the top and sides.

Heart or triangular shaped faces need side or forward bangs with some fullness on the sides.

Oval shaped faces style-wise can do just about anything. That is why the oval has the perfect shaped face.

Nails

Manicured nails are critical for a man. The hands are the most visible part of the body. We shake hands, demonstrate equipment, pass paperwork and talk with our hands.

I recommend men have a manicure. The manicurist will trim your nails and cuticles, moisturize and buff the nails. You will feel so much better about the appearance of your hands and others will notice how well groomed you are. Grooming is a fine detail. When you pay attention to fine details in your appearance you will also pay attention to details in your work. Grooming is a critical piece of the professional appearance package. Many people do not take the time to pay attention to their skin care, hygiene, nails and hair. When an individual is groomed, he looks and feels better. Feeling good is what it is all about. When you look good, you feel good which builds self esteem and confidence.

Chapter Ten

Grooming for the Professional Woman

Personal hygiene is important in the care of our bodies. Bathing or showering everyday should be standard practice, along with regular doctor and dentist visits, eating and exercising properly. Drink plenty of water. Water helps moisturize and purify the skin. Water also helps us maintain or lose weight.

Water helps moisturize and purify the skin— it also helps us maintain or lose weight.

Skin care

It is important for women to utilize a three-step basic skin care program of **cleansing lotion** (not soap), **freshener** and **moisturizer**. The cleansing lotion will wash off your make-up or dirt from the day. Soap is drying to the skin and that speeds up the aging process. After you wash your face you have altered the pH and acid balance and opened up your pores. It is important to use a freshener to close the pores and balance the skin. Use a moisturizer developed especially for your face. As the skin dries with age, it will need more moisturizing emollients. If you are using a moisturizer on your face and find yourself using more and more, that is a sign that it is time to move to a stronger moisturizer that has more of the emollients your skin needs at that time of your life. If the moisturizer is working, you only need a drop the size of a dime to cover the whole face.

The only other skin care step a woman needs to follow is to use a scrub or a masque to deep cleanse the skin. A deep cleanser or exfoliant cleans the second and third layer of the skin. Cleansing lotion only cleans the top layer of skin. If your skin type is **normal**, use the deep cleanser once a week. If your skin type is **oily**, use the deep cleanser twice a week. If you use a deep cleanser too often, you activate the oil glands and find yourself needing to cleanse more. If this is the case, only deep cleanse twice a week. The oil glands will eventually slow down. For skin that is **dry**, deep cleanse one to two times a month.

Make-up

Make-up is an essential piece of the professional woman's appearance package.

Make-up is an essential part of the professional woman's appearance package. Make-up completes the professional woman's appearance. Make-up should look and feel very fresh and natural. The key is to wear the right color make-up, apply according to your facial features and blend, blend, blend. Make-up for the professional woman is foundation, blush, lipstick and mascara. Lipstick is essential. You can have no make-up on but lipstick and look like you completed your face. You can have full make-up on but no lipstick and look like you

The key is to wear the right color make-up, apply according to your facial features and blend, blend, blend.

have nothing on. Go through a make-up lesson with a trained technician.

Beware, most of the make-up counter technicians have no training in what colors work best for you and what your personality is. They are trained to know ingredients in products and how to sell. Therefore, use your own good judgment and knowledge on appropriate colors to purchase. If you are the least bit unsure, do not buy the products.

Naturals like little make-up. **Classics** like make-up simple and controlled. **Romantics** and **Dramatics** enjoy wearing make-up and need to watch that it is toned down and appears fresh and natural.

Cools need a rose base in their foundation, blush and lipsticks. **Warms** need a brown base in their foundation, blush and lipsticks. The correct make-up colors will enhance your skin undertone, blend easily and will give you a healthy appearance.

Hair

Hair can make or break a woman's professional appearance. The most professional length is at least one inch off the shoulders, especially after we reach twenty-five years of age. If you are younger, pull your hair back and up in a professional style for work. Play with your hair in the mirror and look at the message you send when your hair is down and flowing as

If you are the least bit unsure of a make-up color, do not buy the products.

opposed to up in a nice style. A good stylist should be able to give you a style for casual, work and evening all in one cut. It is important to communicate the following information to your stylist to obtain the best cut and style for you.

Hair color needs to appear natural. No one but yourself should be able to tell when it is time to color your hair again. Cosmetologists usually have no training to be able to look at you and determine your skin undertone. Communicate this information to your stylist to receive the correct hair color.

Cools: Mixing blue and violet is the key in hair color; blonde shades need to be an ash blonde (ash has gray in it), red shades need to be a slight hint of burgundy or eggplant.

Warms: mixing gold and orange is the key in hair color; blond shades need to be a golden blonde (golden has beige in it), red shades need to be an orange or strawberry red.

Use the following checklist to communicate to your stylist your ability to work with your hair, the texture of your hair, the shape of your face along with your personality.

Personality:

☐ **Natural** means you do not want to fuss with your hair, you want a wash and wear hair style.

☐ **Classic** means you will use a blow dryer or lightly use the curling iron. It is important to you that your hair looks styled and controlled.

☐ **Romantic** you will fuss with your hair and like the soft look.

☐ **Dramatic** you like to experiment with your hair and like the angular look.

Ability to work with your hair:

☐ excellent ☐ good ☐ fair ☐ poor

Texture of your hair:

☐ thick ☐ thin ☐ course ☐ fine

Shape of your face:

☐ round

☐ square

☐ oblong or rectangular

☐ heart or triangular

☐ oval

*Manicured
nails are
important
to the
professional
woman. You
can hide your
hips but you
cannot hide
your hands.*

Round, you need your hair styled back away from your face.

Square, you need softness and curves styled in your hair.

Oblong/rectangular, you need some fullness on the top and sides.

Heart/triangular, you need side or forward bangs with the hair styled into the cheek area.

Oval shaped faces style-wise can do anything. We call this the perfect shaped face.

Nails

Manicured nails are important to the professional woman. Nails are the most visible part of the body. You can hide your hips but you cannot hide your hands. Have your nails manicured or do it yourself on a regular basis. **Naturals** will not want polish and that is fine. **Classics, Romantics** and **Dramatics** will enjoy wearing polish.

Make sure the nail polish color complements you and is neutral looking. Cools look good in blue reds, roses and pinks. Warms look attractive in tomato red, corals, oranges, browns.

Do not wear funky, trendy colors or designs. The nail polish should never be loud or distracting. The business length for nails is 1/4".

Grooming is a critical piece of the professional appearance package. Many people do not take the time to pay attention to their skin care, make-up, hygiene, nails and hair. When a woman is groomed, she looks and feels better. Feeling good is what it is all about. When you look good, you feel good which builds self esteem and confidence.

Chapter Eleven

You Need to Have a Plan

Wardrobe Planning for the Professional Person

Seventy percent of your closet should be your professional or work wardrobe. This is a separate wardrobe from your casual or evening attire. Check this **Basic Professional Wardrobe Plan** against what is in your existing closet. First, separate your professional wardrobe from your casual and evening attire.

The secret to looking professional is keeping your work wardrobe separate from your casual or evening wardrobe. Even in a business casual atmosphere, those business casual clothes should not be worn outside of work.

If you are in a **power professional** position or industry, you will then have more business suits and less business casual clothes. If you are in a **business casual** work environment, you will have fewer business suits.

For men or women in a **professional** position, the men will have more suits with different color jacket and trouser combinations and the women different color jackets with trousers, dresses or skirt combinations.

The secret to looking professional is keeping your work wardrobe separate from your casual or evening wardrobe.

If you have not worn an item of clothing in a year, you will NOT wear it.

Before you check this professional wardrobe plan against your closet, go through your closet and separate your **wearable** clothing from the **repairable** clothes and **discards**. The clothes you can wear should remain in the closet. Put the items that need repair in a pile. The repairable items are clothes that need a button, zipper, snap fixed, etc. Make a pile for the discards. The discards are clothes you have not worn in a year. Put these clothes in a bag or box and give them to a charity.

If you have not worn an item of clothing in a year, you will NOT wear it even if you think you will. No excuses...if I lose weight or maybe I will wear it. If you have a hard time letting go of things, put the discards in a box and put them in the attic, closet or garage. What will happen is you won't miss those clothes and will finally give them away.

As you go through your professional wardrobe update, take out a piece of paper and make a list of the items you need to buy. You will be developing a shopping plan for yourself.

Basic Professional Wardrobe Plan for Men

Use your color chart to choose colors.

Shoes 2 pairs

☐ Black, plain or textured, slip-on or tie shoe

☐ Violet/Red/Rose = burgundy

☐ Golden/Orange/Tawny = brown

Belts 2 Smooth or Textured leather

☐ Violet/Red/Rose = black or burgundy with silver buckle

☐ Golden/Orange/Tawny = navy or brown with a gold buckle

Socks   12 pairs

☐ Violet/Red/Rose = black

☐ Golden/Orange/Tawny = dark brown

Ties 3 per suit

☐ 100% silk is the best tie fabric. Pattern choice will depend on your personality type as described in the chapter on Personality.

Coats

☐ Topcoat
Zip-out liner if you live in a cold climate
Violet/Red = black, gray, burgundy
Rose = burgundy, gray or dark navy
Golden/Orange/Tawny = camel, rust, brown

Suits   5

☐ 2 in your dark neutral

☐ 2 in medium neutral

☐ 1 in light neutral

Violet/Red =   black, charcoal, gray, navy, taupe or blue

Rose = charcoal, gray, navy, slate blue, federal blue

Golden/Orange = brown, navy, warm gray, camel, light blue

Tawny = dark brown, medium brown, rust, olive green, camel

Business Social Attire

☐ Use your darkest neutral suit

☐ Smooth shoe

☐ Cotton/polyester blend shirt with a regular collar

☐ Socks, over the calf

Personal Wear

☐ 12 underwear

☐ 12 handkerchiefs

☐ 3 pocket handkerchief* (*only if you enjoy wearing these)

Business Casual

☐ 3 slacks

☐ 3 golf shirts

☐ 4 shirts: solid, print, plaid, checks, stripes with button down or standard collar, long or short sleeve

☐ Sweaters: 2 cardigan, 2 crew neck

Sport Coats

☐ 2 blazers

Slacks 2 per sport coat

☐ Solid, textured, or patterned will depend on your personality (see chapter on Personality)

Dress Shirts   5 per suit

☐ 3 plain or tone on tone cotton/polyester blend with a regular collar

Violet/Red = white

Rose = off white

Golden/Orange = cream

Tawny = beige

☐ 2 light color with or without a striped pattern

Professional Accessories

Follow your shoe color choices.

☐ Appointment book

☐ Briefcase

☐ Leather pad

☐ Gold or silver pen

Violet/Red/Rose = silver

Golden/Orange/Tawny = gold

Jewelry

☐ Watch: silver, gold or leather band in one of your colors

Keep your jewelry simple and controlled. You can still bring in your personality (see chapter on Personality).

Gloves

☐ Match your coat color.

Once you have your basic wardrobe in place, replace an article of clothing as it wears out. Your lifestyle will change about every three years. It is a good idea every three years to take out a piece of paper and for a period of about two weeks, twenty-four hours a day, three times that year, write down where you went, what you wore and what you wish you had worn.

For example: Sunday morning put on my shabby robe to have breakfast and read the paper. Wish I had a new robe with no holes in it. From this exercise you will develop a shopping plan of items of clothing you need to replace. It is much easier to shop when you know exactly what you are shopping for.

Your lifestyle will change about every three years.

Every three years take out a piece of paper and for a period of about two weeks, twenty-four hours a day, three times that year, write down where you went, what you wore and what you wish you had worn.

A Basic Professional Wardrobe Plan
for Women

Use your color chart to choose colors.

Coats 1 each

☐ Basic, long enough to cover your skirt and dress hemlines

☐ Raincoat (a zip-out lining is best for those who live in a colder climate)

Neutral color choices

Violet/Red = black, gray, burgundy

Rose = gray, burgundy, navy

Golden/Orange = brown, camel, navy

Tawny = dark brown, rust, olive

Basic Skirt Suit

☐ 3 for winter of wool or a blend, lined

☐ 3 for summer of a blend, lined

☐ or 6 made of an all year round fabric

Basic Dress

☐ 2 classic style, no pattern your neutral color (see color choices from above)

☐ 1 dress in your colors with a pattern that represents your personality (see chapter on Personality).

Long sleeve dresses are recommended. Adding one plain and one patterned dress with short sleeves is optional.

Professional Coordinates

☐ 3 skirts the proper length in your neutral colors

☐ 6 long sleeve blouses made of a cotton/ polyester blend or silk

☐ 3 short sleeve blouses made of cotton/ polyester blend or silk

☐ 3-4 jackets that can be worn with skirt, blouse or dress coordinates

Pant Suit

☐ 1 in your neutral color

☐ 1 in your basic or bright color

Violet = fuschia, red, teal, royal blue

Red = taupe, navy, red

Rose = mauve, federal blue, soft green

Golden/Orange = royal blue, green

Tawny = camel, rust or sage green

If you choose a fabric that can be worn all year, you only need two pant suits. If you choose a winter fabric and a summer fabric, you should have four pant suits.

Business Social

☐ 1 business suit worn with dressy accessories, or

☐ 1 of your business dresses worn with dressy accessories, or

☐ 1 long sleeve silk blouse with a skirt

☐ 1 evening dress*

(*not see-through, low-cut, off the shoulders or slits longer than six inches, keep hemline professional)

Business Casual

☐ 1 long sleeve dress

☐ 1 short sleeve dress

☐ 2 -3 cotton blend blouses

☐ 2 -3 tops

☐ 3 trouser style slacks

☐ 3 sweaters, 1 long sleeve cardigan

Shoes

☐ 2 basic closed pumps with a 1"-2" heel

☐ 2 flat shoes

Professional Accessories

Follow your shoe color choices.

☐ Appointment book

☐ Briefcase

☐ Leather pad

☐ Gold or silver pen

     Violet/Red/Rose = silver

     Golden/Orange/Tawny = gold

Jewelry

☐ Pearl necklace and earrings

☐ Watch: silver, gold or leather band in one of your colors

☐ 3 pins

☐ 3 necklaces

☐ 6 pairs of earrings

Keep your jewelry simple and controlled. You can still bring in your personality (see chapter on Personality).

Gloves

☐ Match your coat color.

Intimate Apparel

☐ 3 bras

☐ 3 slips if suits, skirts or dresses not lined

☐ 6 panties

☐ 6 pairs hosiery of one shade

Nude color hosiery works for everyone.

Violet/Red/Rose = taupe/gray

Golden/Orange/Tawny = suntan/beige

Once you have your basic wardrobe in place, as an article of clothing wears out, then replace it. Your lifestyle will change about every three years. It is a good idea every three years to take out a piece of paper and for two weeks, twenty-four hours a day, three times that year, write down where you went, what you wore and what you wish you had worn.

For example: Sunday morning put on my shabby robe to have breakfast and read the paper. Wish I had a new robe with no holes in it. From this exercise you will develop a shopping plan of items of clothing you need to replace. It is much easier to shop when you know exactly what you are shopping for.

Every three years take out a piece of paper and for a period of about two weeks, twenty-four hours a day, three times that year, write down where you went, what you wore and what you wish you had worn.

Your lifestyle will change about every three years.

Chapter Twelve

Putting It All Together

Your goal over the next year to two years is to eliminate those items of clothing or accessories that do not work the **best** for you. If an article of clothing or accessory has not been worn in a year, it will not be worn. Put it in a box and give it away.

To look your professional best is about being authentically you through your wardrobe, grooming and accessories.

When shopping, follow these rules:

1) Only buy the colors which complement your skin undertone.

2) Only buy the style which complements your body structure.

3) Only buy clothes with textures and patterns you **love**, not just like.

4) Sit in the outfit at the store to make sure nothing pulls or bags.

5) Look in a full length mirror from the sides, back and front to make sure everything lays neat and flat.

6) Does the article of clothing or outfit send the message you are looking to accomplish: power professional, professional, or business casual?

*Keep attuned
to the fact that
your coloring,
body structure
and personality
do not change.*

7) Is the outfit professional and appropriate for the workplace?

8) Do you need this article of clothing or is it already in your closet?

9) Make sure the material is a good quality blend.

10) Can you wear this article of clothing all year round or only seasonally?

*Lifestyle will
change about
every three
years and
can dictate
wardrobe
changes.*

11) Keep within your budget, it is not how much you spend but how wisely you invest your money to look professional. Remember, it is the cost per wearing that counts not the original cost of the item.

12) If the outfit is wrinkled in the store, it will be difficult to iron; do not buy it.

13) Beware of sales, usually a sale item is one you will not wear.

14) Stay away from trends and fads.

15) Do have an updated appearance.

16) Only go with current fashion if the item is your color, style, texture and pattern. If it is missing in just one area, you will not wear it and it will be a waste of money.

17) Shop alone so you can concentrate on your goals.

18) Do not let anyone talk you into buying anything.

19) Dress well when shopping to gain respect and service.

20) Wear the appropriate shoes or bring them with you to slip on with the outfits you try on.

21) Have your shopping list with you to avoid impulse buying.

22) Ask yourself, does this outfit work in my job and does it represent the image I want to project?

Keep attuned to the fact that your coloring, body structure and personality do not change. Lifestyle will change about every three years and can dictate wardrobe changes. Examples of possible lifestyle changes: married or single, type of industry you work in, level of position, geographic area, children and age.

❖

Chapter Thirteen

So What is Business Casual?

This is the million dollar question in the business world. Years ago men and women wore uniforms on the job. Employees complained about the uniform. Then the business world dictated men and women wear a dark navy business suit with white shirt/blouse with a red tie/bow. Employees felt restricted in this attire. Today professional dress has gotten lost and you cannot tell who the professional is or who the customer, client or patient is anymore.

An interesting fact is many of the companies who have tried to implement one day to five days of business casual have found more disadvantages than benefits. Why? Employees either do not understand what business casual is or they do not want to dress business casual. As I train in more and more companies, I am surprised at the number of employees who approach me to share their dislike of business casual and their wish that managers implement a guideline for professional dress.

Companies who have implemented business casual have found more disadvantages than benefits.

Employees do not understand what business casual is.

*Most employees do **not** want to dress business casual.*

Just as there are different levels of dress (power professional, professional and business casual), there are levels of dress within business casual. Consider what your profession is and what the image is you want to project to those around you. For example: I attend a national convention every year and the dress is business casual. Those presenters, introducers and anyone in front of the audience should not be dressed business casual. Their attire is power professional. Anyone who represents an organization as an officer such as a chapter president should be dressed professionally and not business casual.

Rule: Always dress one level higher to gain respect and be remembered for the professional you are and work so hard to be. Have a separate wardrobe for business casual. Do not wear any of these clothes for casual wear. Keep this wardrobe for work only. Here are the different levels of business casual.

Men

Level 1:

This level is the most common business casual.

- Sport coat
- Medium to dark colored, long or short shirt with a collar
- Tie
- Cotton, pleated style pants
- Loafer shoes

Level 2:

The above outfit with the tie and/or sport coat removed.

Level 3:

- Golf, banded or collared shirt
- Cotton, pleated style pants
- Loafer shoes

Level 4:

- No-collar shirt, crew neck
- Cotton, pleated style pants
- Tennis shoes

Level 5:

- Crew neck shirt

- Jeans

- Tennis shoes

Guidelines for men: Fun cotton shirts should be left at home. If your company has a "support your local sport team for a day," wear the supporting sport shirt only that day.

Men should always wear socks. If your company is level 5 then have a specific pair of tennis shoes and jeans to be worn for work only. You will actually save money by having a separate pair of tennis shoes and jeans from the at-home tennis shoes and jeans.

Women

Level 1:

- Business blouse, short or long sleeve

- Trouser style pants

- Jacket

- Flat closed-in shoes

Level 2:

- Business blouse, short or long sleeve
- Trouser style pants
- Flat closed-in shoes

Level 3:

- Pants outfit
- Flat closed-in shoes

Level 4:

- Collared top
- Cotton, pleated pants
- Flat shoes

Level 5:

- Crew neck top
- Cotton pleated style pants
- Flat shoes or tennis shoes

Level 6:

- Crew neck top
- Jeans
- Tennis shoes

Guidelines for women: Wear hosiery with levels 1 through 4 and socks with levels 5 and 6. No stirrup pants. Have a specific pair of tennis shoes and jeans to be worn for work. You will save money by having separate tennis shoes and jeans, from the at-home tennis shoes and jeans.

Think about these things before you pick out your business casual attire.

- The type of profession you are in.

- Your position with the company.

- The type of clients you have.

- The position you strive for within the company.

- The image you want to project.

Dress one level higher and you will always feel comfortable and gain respect from those around you.

A company or individual should never have to apologize for dressing business casual, as long as business casual dress is done correctly. Dress one level higher and you will always feel comfortable. You will gain the respect of those people around you as a result of the professional image you project.

Dilbert reprinted by permission of United Feature Syndicate, Inc.

Taking Casual Fridays Seriously, Pros Say Go With Black Separates

By Eileen Kinsella
Staff Reporter of The Wall Street Journal

Apparently, knowing how to dress down for the office can be every bit as anxiety-producing as knowing how to dress up.

A recent memo distributed to Hearst Magazines employees at the company's New York headquarters announced that "casual Fridays" had been extended indefinitely after a successful trial period this summer. Attached was a sheet with do's and don'ts for the sartorially impaired.

Drawing on the company's reservoir of experts, the memo includes suggestions by fashion editors of various Hearst magazines, including Cosmopolitan, Redbook and Marie Claire. "We thought employees would get a kick out of it," says a Hearst representative.

The memo enthusiastically counsels employees to "Go with casual comfort. It's in." Specific suggestions include: "Look at Casual Fridays as a good opportunity to experiment with a new fragrance" and "Go with black separates—you'll automatically look pulled-together and chic!"

The memo goes on: "For men who won't leave home without a tie, try a knit or a novelty print."

Rather than eschewing suits altogether, Robin Page of Marie Claire suggests: "Ease it up with a banded-collar shirt, or a knit polo for men, or an elegant T-shirt for women. Also, remember that casual doesn't mean sloppy; well-pressed means well-dressed."

Elissa Santisi of Harper's Bazaar says "Pull out the wardrobe items that mean *casual*, but still look professional. Add a classic blue blazer, or a stylish sweater for a touch of sophistication."

John Mather of Esquire adds: "Always base your look on a tailored sport jacket. Pay attention to footwear—no sneakers."

The reaction among workers seems to range from shrugs to mild amusement. One Hearst employee says that since the company never had a strict dress code, the declaration of "casual" for Friday doesn't make much difference in the way most employees come to work.

But during the summer trial period, management took no chances. Each Friday, a sign was posted in the reception areas of the various magazines stating that employees were "currently enjoying a casual day," presumably to assure unwary visitors that they weren't being treated with disrespect. According to one employee, however, someone begged to differ. He or she inserted the word "not" before "enjoying."

Chapter Fourteen

Tattoos, Earrings, Body Piercing, Trends and Fads

There is always something new happening in the world. Or is there? Tattoos, earrings, body piercing, trends and fads—none of these things are really new. They have been around since ancient times. The question is what to do?

Trends and fads have no place in the workplace. There is a difference in being updated in your appearance or wearing a trend or fad. Trends or fads are here today and gone tomorrow. If you are ever unsure, do not buy that trendy article of clothing or accessory as a part of your professional wardrobe.

Image is perception. How do you want to be perceived?

Earrings for men and women need to be simple. Jewelry needs to be conservative yet represent your personality. Simple is the key word.

Do your homework on the policy of the company regarding the number of earrings and types of earrings for men and women. When in doubt, women wear one set of earrings and men wear no earrings. Depending on the policy of the company, your industry and type of clients or customers, two sets of earrings for women and one simple studded earring for men may be acceptable.

Abiding by the company policy or the client's dress ethics shows respect not only for the company or client but respect for yourself as a person. Normally, I wear two sets of simple earrings. When I train for the Ritz-Carlton I only wear one set of earrings because that is their policy.

Tattoos and body piercing are very personal choices and can be credibility robbers to your professional image. To be safe, since none of us knows where we will be, what we will do or where our profession could take us, make sure any tattoos and body piercings **cannot** be seen when you are wearing professional attire.

Does the picture of the woman on the back of this book appear to be someone you would imagine to have tattoos? People are shocked to find out that, yes, I have numerous tattoos. One is the size of this book on my right hip. Another is pictured on the next page. Thank you to Gregory Christian, my son, for his excellent artwork.

Image is perception. How do you want to be perceived? How you present yourself to others is the key to how you will be received.

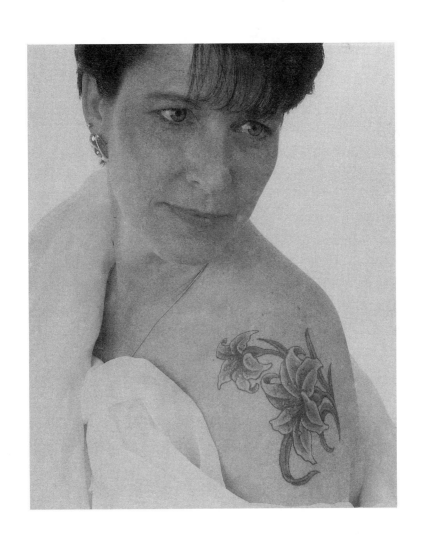

Chapter Fifteen

Professionalism, Promotion, and Profit

Projecting your **best** professional appearance is one hundred percent beneficial. There are no negatives when you present **your best** image. Image development is a learned skill like any other academic skill we are taught.

Image development is a learned skill.

Once you have gone through your own personal full image consultation and learned what works best for you in color, style, textures and patterns, you know the process forever. The reason for this is your coloring and body structure do not change. Once you are past twenty-five years of age, your personality in textures, patterns, accessories and hairstyles changes only slightly. After you build your professional wardrobe around your **best** colors, styles, textures, patterns, accessories and grooming techniques, you will see positive results.

Purchase a full length mirror.

Everyday use the checklist at the end of this chapter and check out your appearance package from head to toe. If everything in the mirror

*If you are
unsure of an
article of
clothing or
accessory, do
not wear it.*

*You will save
yourself time
getting dressed
and time going
shopping.*

*It will take little
effort to get
dressed and you
will save
thousands of
dollars on your
wardrobe
investment.*

*Your
appearance
will help you
be the **best**
professional
you can be!*

checks out and **you look your best**, great, go about your day. If you are unsure about an article of clothing or accessory, do **not** wear it.

Do a wardrobe update once every three years to keep up with the lifestyle changes we tend to go through in that time frame. Use the checklist to work towards accomplishing all the tips from head to toe everyday.

Eventually this process will be like getting up in the morning and brushing your teeth. The process will become routine and you will not have to think about it.

Going through a personal full image development consultation and using the checklist everyday guarantees you will save yourself time getting dressed and time going shopping. It will take little effort to get dressed and you will save thousands of dollars on your wardrobe investment.

Your credibility will increase, you will be more productive (you can concentrate on your job and not on what you are wearing), you will gain respect, recognition and, yes, you will make more money. By projecting your **best** professional image you immediately radiate a trust and comfort level to other people. You will have a higher self esteem and confidence level.

Your appearance will help you be the **best** professional you can be. Today, employers are looking for employees who know their area of expertise, whose appearance is professional, who interact professionally, speak with respect and always have on their professional hat.

*Through image development you will gain **professionalism, promotion** and **profit!***

An image that works for you projects credibility. Credibility brings success. Through image development you will gain **professionalism**, **promotion** and **profit** in your career!

Professional Image Development Checklist

Goal: To check off every box every day.

☐ **Hair:**
Professional style and appropriate length.

☐ **Hair**:
Style complements face shape and personality.

☐ **Hair:**
Color enhances skin undertone and looks natural.

☐ **Hygiene**:
Hair and body are clean.

☐ **Men**:
Facial hair is clean, trimmed, complements face shape & type of industry.

☐ **Women**:
Wearing well blended foundation, blush, lipstick in your complementary colors.

☐ **Jewelry**:
Basic and appropriate for professional position.

☐ **Attire**:
Appropriate for type of industry, position and age.

☐ **Style**:
Attire complements body structure and height.

☐ **Attire**:
Tailored to body structure and appropriate for the business world.

☐ **Wardrobe and accessories**:
Colors which enhance skin undertone.

☐ **Hosiery**:
Is worn and is appropriate color.

☐ **Shoes**:
Clean, right heel height, scuff free and correct color.

☐ **Texture**:
Materials represent personality and appropriate in the work place.

☐ **Patterns**:
Represent personality, in proportion to body structure and appropriate for profession type.

☐ **Nails**:
Well manicured and appropriate length.

Women: Subtle polish color complementary to skin undertone.

☐ **Cologne or perfume**:
Wear none or very little.

☐ **Level of dress**:
Dress according to what the day requires. (Power Professional, Professional or Business Casual)

☐ **Accessories**:
Clean, not scuffed and scaled to body proportions.

☐ **Women**:
Carrying a professional accessory and not a purse.

☐ **Pen**:
Carry a silver or gold pen.

☐ **Glasses**:
Complement you in color, size and shape.

☐ **Trends**:
Do not wear a trend or fad.

☐ **Suit jacket**:
Wear long sleeves for meetings or presentations.

☐ **Women**:
Coat covers your skirt or dress hemline.

Index

ISBN 0-9655742-3-7

Order Form

Best Impressions: How to Gain Professionalism, Promotion and Profit

Placing Your Order

Best Impressions:
How to Gain Professionalism, Promotion and Profit

$16.95 each X _____ books =

$

Sales Tax

Ohio residents add 7% sales tax

$

Shipping

Book Rate: $2.00 first book and 75¢ for each additional book.
($3.50 air mail) Ground shipping may take three to four weeks.

$

TOTAL

$

Payment

☐ **Money Order** ☐ **Master Card** ☐ **Visa** ☐ **American Express**

Card Number: _____

Name on Card: _____ Exp. Date: _____

Signature: _____

Ship To

Company Name: _____

Name: _____

Address: _____

City: _____ State: _____ Zip: _____

Telephone: _____

Please send me information on your ☐ **seminars** ☐ **training programs**

How To Order

 Fax

(440) 572-9145

 Phone

(440) 572-1890
1-888-577-BEST
(2378)

 Mail

Best Impressions®
17749 Lexington Lane
Strongsville, Ohio 44136-7086

ISBN 0-9655742-3-7

Order Form

Best Impressions: How to Gain Professionalism, Promotion and Profit

Placing Your Order

Best Impressions:
How to Gain Professionalism, Promotion and Profit
$16.95 each X _____ books =

$ _____

Sales Tax

Ohio residents add 7% sales tax

$ _____

Shipping

Book Rate: $2.00 first book and 75¢ for each additional book.
($3.50 air mail) Ground shipping may take three to four weeks.

$ _____

TOTAL

$ _____

Payment

☐ **Money Order**   ☐ **Master Card**   ☐ **Visa**   ☐ **American Express**

Card Number: _____

Name on Card: _____ Exp. Date: _____

Signature: _____

Ship To

Company Name: _____

Name: _____

Address: _____

City: _____ State: _____ Zip: _____

Telephone: _____

Please send me information on your ☐ **seminars** ☐ **training programs**

How To Order

 Fax

(440) 572-9145

 Phone

(440) 572-1890
1-888-577-BEST
(2378)

 Mail

Best Impressions®
17749 Lexington Lane
Strongsville, Ohio 44136-7086